SPIKEY

By: William Bennett

Big Bear Publishing
Seattle, WA

First, I would like to give a huge thank you to my wife. Your relentless encouragement is the reason this book is out today. I would like to give out credit to some amazing people.

Copy Editor: Maxwell Anderson

Illustration by Olga Žuravļova

Cover Design: William C. Bennett

Cover Illustration by Olga Žuravļova

Illustration and Cover copyright 2019 Wilcole Education, LLC

Copyright © 2019 Big Bear Publishing
an imprint of Wilcole Education, LLC

Big Bear Publishing
PO Box 4766
Seattle, WA 98194 U.S.A.
www.bigbearpublishers.com

Printed in the United States of America

The Author

William Bennett is an Educator and an author from the San Francisco Bay Area in California. He spent over a decade teaching English to young learners in Hong Kong. As a creative with a penchant for storytelling and inspiring young learners, William had always wanted to write a book, and the realization of this ambition stands out as one of his greatest achievements.

SPIKEY

The Light

My eyes opened and bright light flooded in. I began to adjust to this new phenomenon. Staring at me was a beautiful, golden dog. My Mom! Next to me were seven siblings. We lay there as our Mom fed us and licked us clean.

I heard a voice calling, "Brandy! Brandy!" As the voice got louder, Mom hid us and revealed herself to the person behind the voice. Mom got some food, some water and even an ear massage. The person really seemed to care for her.

They would appear every day at the same time, and Mom would always hide us from view. I wondered why we couldn't come out. "Never mind," said one of my siblings. "Hurry up. Let's play!" We played, pushed each other around and climbed all over each other while Mom lay there watching us. We had great fun.

One day when Mom was out, the voice returned. My siblings and I tried to hide as we had with Mom. The voice drew nearer and stopped. Suddenly, a man poked his head under Mom's bed where the eight of us were huddled.

He screamed out Mom's name in rage. "BRANDY! " Mom came to the voice. When she arrived, my siblings and I ran to her. The man stared at Mom and us. He was very angry and left the room. Mom looked scared but said that everything would be okay.

Then, the man came back with a box. He picked up Mom and placed her inside. Next, he added my siblings and me. We looked up at him in fear, but Mom licked us over and over, over and over, until we were calm. We wondered where we were going. The man took us outside and placed us on top of a shiny thing with circle feet.

The sun was very hot, so Mom covered us with her body. Soon, the man returned and put us in the shiny thing's belly. What was this thing? We traveled for a while before coming to a stop.

My brothers and sisters and I climbed onto Mom to see what was happening. Outside, I saw a giant box next to the shiny thing.

The man came and picked up the box that held us. He put us inside the giant one, as Mom looked at him with a sad face. The man said two words to Mom: "Bad dog". Then, he went away.

Mom tried to run after the shiny thing, but it faded into the distance. How fast those circle-feet were! Later, Mom returned to the giant box and snuggled us to sleep.

The Giant Box

The giant box smelled strange, and the sun seemed angry; it was extra bright and hot. Mom lifted our spirits with milk. She peeked out from the giant box to see if the man was back, but there was no sign of him. His voice was gone.

Day turned to night and night back to day—over and over again. There were sunny days, rainy days and days with nothing at all. Sometimes, Mom looked at us and smiled. When she did that, we knew that everything was alright.

No matter the weather, Mom would venture out each day to search for food. Often, none could be found, but she never let us sleep without milk. Mom had been a fit and healthy dog, until we got to the big box.

Even without having eaten for days, she had managed to give us milk. Now, I know that this had made her weak. Mom continued to nourish us until she could no longer move.

We tried to play with Mom, but it was no use. She was very thin, and her bones pushed out like sticks. All she could do was lie there helplessly.

One morning, we heard some voices approaching the big box. The voices got closer and closer. Then, a woman was looking down at us. With a smile on her face, she lifted us out of the giant box and carried us away. We all were happy to leave that place.

The woman patted our heads and said, "My name is Catherine. I'll care for you now."

The Big House

Catherine had a shiny thing too, but its feet didn't go so fast. Eventually, it came to a stop beside a very big house. We could hear other dogs barking from in there. Was it a good place?

Catherine came around, picked up our box and took us inside the big house. As we made our way through its halls, we saw many kinds of dogs- big and small.

At last, Catherine took us into a room that was nice and quiet. Another woman brought Mom a big plate of food. Slowly, Mom ate a small portion, unable to finish it all. Next, us young ones ate. The women would bring food for Mom and the rest of us every day, but Mom's body was still too skinny, and she could barely move.

My siblings and I would run around the room to entertain ourselves. We could not go to other parts of the big house. There were big, mean dogs who barked at anything and everything that moved. Sometimes, Catherine would have to soothe them with her friendly voice.

Catherine had many people come to visit us. She said that she wanted us to have a home with a family that would love and take care of us. Each day, new visitors would come to the big house, and sometimes they would leave with one of my siblings.

Catherine said that they were going to a loving home and, in the end, someone would give me a loving home too. Days turned into weeks, and I watched four of my siblings leave the big house. I wished that someone would come and give me a loving home too.

Early one morning, a man came to the big house. He picked me up and said, "I will call you Spikey." The man talked to Catherine about my Mom and me. Mom still looked thin and weak. I wondered if Mom and I would be going with this man, but off he went alone. We pups returned to our games and Mom her rest.

Several weeks later, the man returned. He wrapped me in his arms and said, "Come on. We're going home." Catherine and the other woman each cuddled me, saying goodbye and best of luck.

A big, shiny circle-foot pulled up next to the big house, and the man said, "This is my car." Inside, there was another man who looked very happy to see me. We sat down, and the 'car' sped off. Goodbye, big house.

New Family

The ride from the big house was very long. The man had me sit on the seat of the big car. He looked at me and said, "My name is William, and we are family now." This made me happy, but the big car moved around a lot, and I began to feel funny.

No matter what I did, the sensation wouldn't stop. Then, I felt a strange tug in my belly, and all of my lunch came back out. The big car came to a stop, and William jumped into action, cleaning the mess I had made.

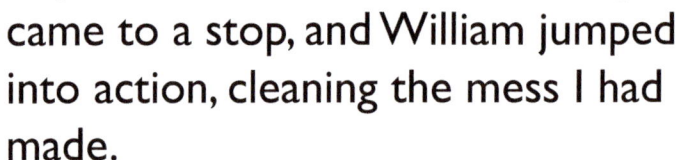

He wasn't even angry! Later, the car came to its last stop. William let me out, and before my eyes were the tallest buildings I'd ever seen. William looked at me and said, "We're almost home now. We live way up there, Spikey."

He held me as he walked to a building with the number eight on its side. We entered the building and waited in front of three doors with buttons between them. One of the doors opened. We entered a box with more buttons on its walls.

William pressed a button and the doors closed. Suddenly, we started moving. What was happening? Who was lifting us up? As fast as the box had begun moving, it stopped. The doors opened, we walked out, and the doors closed.

Then, William opened another door. His house was very high in the sky! I could see so far away but was scared to look down. All I wanted to do was poop. I searched around for a spot but I couldn't find one. I looked and looked, and, finally, I let loose on the floor.

William ran over muttering words I could not understand. He looked at me, and I looked at him with a sad face. William said, "It's okay, buddy," and he went along cleaning up my mess again. I decided to be more careful.

William had a little friend that would always visit him. His name was Ross. He was an interesting, little person. He loved to play with me but would run away whenever I tried to get close to him.

Every time he came over, I would run after him. Sometimes, Ross would throw my toy ball and I would catch it, but, again, he'd run away when I came back with the ball.

William would take the ball and give it to Ross. Over and over, this process repeated, never getting old. Ross loved to grab ahold of my tail. He would chase me around to catch it, and when I turned around, he'd run off screaming. He was fun to have around.

One day, William took out a blue tub. He put a blanket inside and said, "This is your new bed." I jumped into the tub, happily. Wow! It was very soft. I started to scratch the blanket as if I were digging in the sand. I spun around and went to sleep.

The sun went down, the moon showed its face, and I fell into a dream. My Mom and siblings were beside me. I woke up to find myself all alone. I started crying. I missed Mom.

I missed my brothers and sisters. I missed my family, but William heard my crying, and came to me. He patted me down, saying, "It's okay. Everything will be okay. I'm here for you." I looked at him and, feeling safe, fell back asleep.

When the sun showed its face again, William came and picked me up. "Hey, Spikey," he said. "I have a surprise for you!" He pulled out a giant teddy bear and said, "This is yours!" I pounced on the teddy bear like a real hunter. What fun!

As I was playing, William came over and pet me with a smile. I looked at him thinking, 'I like this place.' I was taken cared of. I was loved. He was my family, and I was at home.

The Vet

I loved my new family and loved the big house. I ran all over the house, but there was one area that I didn't like to go. There, you could see far away, but it was too scary. I felt like I was going to fall. I decided to be braver when I was big.

One day, after a night of slumber, I saw William preparing a bag of my toys and snacks. I wondered why he was doing that but carried on playing. William approached me and said, "We're going on a trip, Spikey"! I was super excited. A trip! I was leaving the house! Oh boy! Oh boy! I missed the outside!

William approached me with a leash. I sat down obediently as he secured it to my collar. I sat patiently, waiting for William, but when he turned the handle on the door, I was ready to speed out like a race car. The door opened, and I was off... only to realize the leash was very short! William looked at me and laughed very hard.

We approached the three doors with buttons between them. William pressed a button and waited. I wanted to play. William took off my leash and ran off. I immediately ran after him. Boy, was he fast! William stopped, and one of the three doors opened.

We entered the box with many buttons on the sides. William pressed a button, and I lost my balance. This time, the box was falling, and I couldn't figure out how to stand still.

William smiled at me and said, "You will be okay." The box's door opened, and we walked out. William picked me up, and together we left the building.

William walked with me in his arms for a long time. There were so many people around us, and everyone wanted to touch me. There were many kinds of sounds: some funny, some scary. I tried to walk, but William would not put me down, so I moved a lot in his arms, standing on William's hands to try to see. I saw small cars, big cars, small people and big people.

We arrived at a building with the word 'Vet' on the side. We walked inside, and a woman had me stand on a cold machine. William sat down, and I got to play. I could hear many other animals but could not see them. It drove me crazy! I ran in circles, trying to find out where they were.

One dog came out of a small door next to the woman. The dog was much bigger than me. He ran over to me, but I quickly hid behind William who laughed, asking why I was scared. I don't think that William understood that this dog was big, and I was small. The big dog left the building.

Shortly after, a woman walked in with a bag. I smelled something, but it was not a dog. That must be a cat! A cat! A cat! A cat! My first encounter with a cat! I ran toward the woman with the bag, but William pulled me back. I wanted to see a cat! What did they look like? "

Meow. Meow. Meow." I heard a cat! A cat! A cat! A cat! A man came out and called my name, "Spikey." William picked me up, and we went over to the man. We followed him into a room with lots of funny objects.

Then, in walked a woman who said "Hi Spikey!" 'Everyone is so friendly here,' I thought to myself.

William pet me while talking to the man and woman. The woman petted me and tried to hold me down. I moved from her to William. He gave me a hug and said, "It's okay Spikey," as the man walked over with something in his hand.

I felt a sting like a mosquito had just bitten me. "Good boy," said the man and William. I don't know why they said so, but my tail began to swing. William picked me up, and we left the building.

On our way home, we stopped at a store. This store had all kinds of food and many toys too. Three women at the store started to pet me. They seemed to be very interested in me! William bought some food and a new toy.

The toy looked like a watermelon and smelled like one too. It would turn out to be one of my favorite toys of all time. When we got home, all I could think of was playing with my new watermelon toy... and that's just what I did. I played until the sun said goodnight.

William took me on another trip to see the man inside the vet building. Another sting and we were out of there. This time, William did not carry me in his arms. He let me walk all the way home with him. The walk was exciting and scary at the same time.

There were so many people walking alongside us. There were so many things to see! My head was always turning. Big cars with big sounds passed very close to me. I ran and got closer to William. The walk seemed longer than the first time.

Upon arriving at home, William grabbed my watermelon toy and my water tray. Then, we went outside to a park with many dogs. I was excited to see them. However, I was very scared when they came close to me. I would run off and hide behind William when other dogs came close.

We went to another park where it was just the two of us. William threw my watermelon toy, and I ran after it. William would run, and I would chase him. We played until I was exhausted. Then, we walked back to the house. All I wanted to do was sleep.

William began to walk me every morning and evening. I liked this new routine, I liked to be outside. Days in and days out, we had the same routine. One sunny day, William took me outside. This time, there was a car. We got in and drove away. I wondered where we were going.

We came to this big park, the car stopped, and we got out. It was the biggest park I'd ever seen. William took off my leash, and I ran as far as I could. I had never seen so many trees in my life. So many places to pee! Also, I was able to do something that I couldn't in the house: dig! I dug holes here, there, everywhere.

William had some other people with us. There was one man that loved to have me chase him. We ran and ran and ran. Breathless, I limped over to William and collapsed beside him. William looked at me with a laugh. "Having fun?" he asked.

The weather was scorching, so William poured me a nice cold bowl of water. It was very nice to cool down. After a long day of playing and meeting new friends, we left the big park for home.

There, William poured me some food and fresh water. He sat on the sofa looking at the moving picture box. I climbed onto the sofa and laid on William. He held me very close as I drifted into sweet slumber.

The New Land

had spent months with William in the tall house. I was growing fast, and, for some reason, the house seemed smaller. William brought a magic wall and of me. When I looked at this wall, I could see another dog.

Why were there two dogs here? I barked and ran and hid behind William. I could see William pointing at me saying, "Spikey," and pointing at the other dog in the magic wall saying, "Spikey." William and I played as usual before he left the house.

When William left, I continued playing until I felt tired enough for a nap. Play, sleep, play, sleep. I repeated the process until I heard William opening the door. Normally, he would come in quickly and give me a giant hug. However, this time, William opened the door slowly and told me to sit. I sat as requested, waiting anxiously.

William revealed a giant box with holes in it. I looked at William with my confused face, head moving side to side. What was this holey box and why had William brought it into the house? William closed the door and looked at me. "This is your travel house." I looked at him with my head tilted.

William tried to get me into the giant box, but I would not go in. The box was very scary. I went to investigate the box. I smelled for other dogs, but there was no such scent. I did smell my favorite snacks inside! I had to get them!

The door to the box was open, and I moved cautiously towards the opening. I put one paw in, then a second, then a third. Suddenly, the door started closing. I jumped backward quickly, pushing the door open and exiting the box.

I stopped and stared at it. After all, my snacks were in there. I tried again, one paw at a time. The fourth paw was in and yes! Snacks! Snacks! Snacks! This box was not bad after all. The box was huge. I could stand, sit, move around and even chase my tail. I would spend some time in the box every day, and there were always snacks to be found.

One day, William had a different routine. He took me on a very long walk. I ran, and we played ball, I chased William, and we played hide and seek. After our extended walk, we went home. William packed my snacks, filled the water bottle on the big box. He seemed to be very busy packing many things. When he finished packing, nothing was left in the house. Again, I looked at William with a confused face.

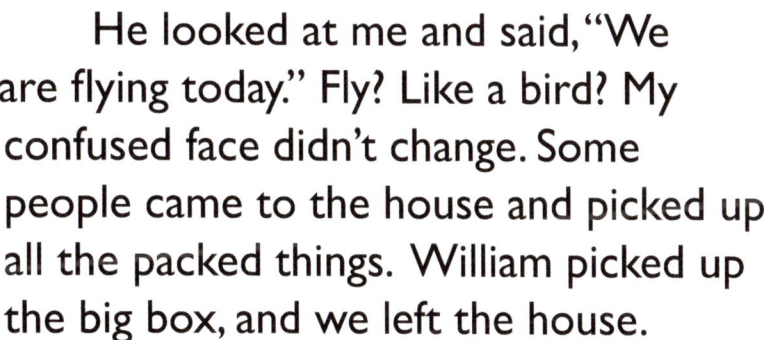

He looked at me and said, "We are flying today." Fly? Like a bird? My confused face didn't change. Some people came to the house and picked up all the packed things. William picked up the big box, and we left the house.

A big car arrived, and we got in. This car ride was different from the others. It was very long, but, even so, I didn't get sick in the car. When the car came to a stop and the doors opened, there were strange things flying in the sky with thunderous sounds. They were like great, big birds.

We entered a colossal building. There were so many people walking around this building. A woman approached William and talked to him. William looked at me and said, "It is time for you to go in your box, Spikey."

The box opened, and I smelled my favorite snacks again. I ran inside to get my snacks, and the door closed. William came to the front of the door on the box. He said, "We are going to fly, and everything will be okay." I still didn't know how dogs could fly, and I was scared. William looked at me with a sad face and said, "I will see you very soon."

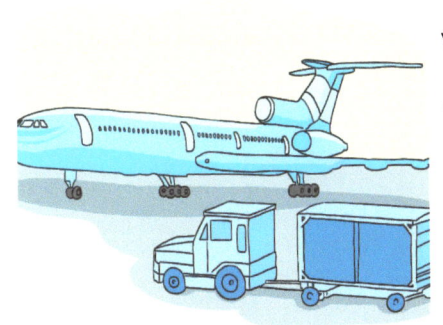

The box began to move, and William waved as I moved further away from him. I stayed in a room for a while, then ended up on in another box that moved. I came to a stop next to one of the great, big birds.

I had never seen a bird so big. How would it fly? For a long time, I waited beside it, and then I heard William's voice. I looked around frantically to find him. Like magic, he showed up right in front of me. "Hey, buddy! How are you? We will be leaving soon, everything will be okay."

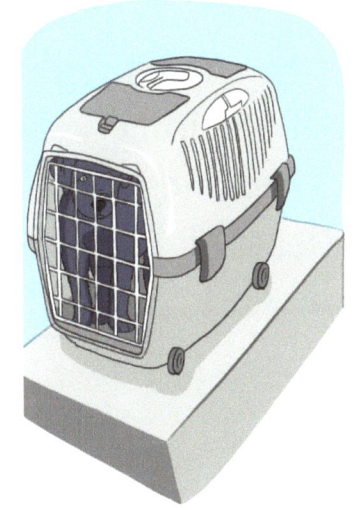

He stuck his hand through the doors to pet me. As quickly as William had appeared, he was gone, and my box started moving again. It got closer to the great, big bird. Two men opened a door in its side and through the door I went!

The door of the great, big bird closed, and it became very dark. The bird started to move but soon stopped. Then, it began to move again, but this time I could feel it was much faster. At this point, I lost my balance and felt like I was floating.

What was happening? Where was William? Why was it so dark in here? I paced around my box until I fell asleep. After a long while in the bird, I felt a bump and I got my balance back. The great, big bird stopped, and the door opened.

Two men came and picked me up and took me out. I was in a strange, new place, and the air was freezing! They moved me into a new building, and right before my eyes stood William! I was so happy to see him. I thought I was going to be in that bird forever.

William and I left the building and entered a car. This time, I was free to move around. William opened the windows of the car, and I stuck my head outside. The cold wind hit my face, and I ducked back in. I tried again, head out the window. This time I enjoyed the wind, and my tongue flapped all over. It was fun!

We arrived at a house where William and I slept. We were both very tired. The next day, William took me to the biggest park in the whole wide world. Everywhere I looked I could see grass! I ran and ran so far away from William. He stood there just watching me as I ran around alone. This new land was fantastic! I knew I was going to love it there, and couldn't wait for what would come next.

San Francisco, California. U.S.A.

SPIKEY

www.ingramcontent.com/pod-product-compliance
Lightning Source LLC
LaVergne TN
LVHW072054070426
835508LV00002B/92